^ZC HORSES
DARBY
THE COW DOG

Diane W. Keaster

illustrated by
Carrie Sigglin
Toni Becker
and
Debbie Page

ISBN 978-0-9721496-8-6

Printed in Canada

ᶻC HORSES
DARBY
THE COW DOG

To Toni and Warren, my good friends who share the same deep love for animals.

^{Z}C HORSES
SERIES

Be part of them all!

Chick - The Beginning!

Chick - The Saddle Horse!

Chick - The Mom!

Luke - The First!

Barbie - The Best!

Leroy - The Stallion!

And Many More!

^ZC HORSES
DARBY
THE COW DOG

TABLE OF CONTENTS

1

PACKING SALT

Being a rancher is an exciting job. In fact, ranching is not really just onc job. Many different jobs make up the profession of ranching. All of the jobs are fun and exciting. They also make you happy knowing you are helping the cows and horses on the ranch.

Fulfilling one job makes cows feel better. This is making sure they have salt to lick. Salt is not normally located in some areas. Salt is a mineral cows need in their bodies. We all need it, too. This job does not involve taking a salt shaker to the cows. A shaker is what we use to get our salt. The salt cows eat comes in square blocks. The block looks like a large sugar cube. In fact, salt is almost like sugar to cows. They love sliding their rough tongues over the salty cube. Horses like it, too. Sometimes they take a big bite out of it.

When cows are in their summer pasture, they need salt packed to them. Often a mountain pasture is too tough to get to in a truck. When this happens, you have to ride horses in to the cows. One horse or two has to be led. These horses pack the salt on a special saddle on their backs. The trip back home is much easier for them. The bulky salt blocks are left on the mountain for the cows. The best part of most of the jobs on a ranch is getting to ride your horse. It is wonderful being able to enjoy the outdoors with this best friend! Another best friend was always at my side when I rode. It did not matter if I was packing salt to the cows, moving them to another pasture, or breaking a young horse. My dog Darby was always at my side. It did not matter what horse I was riding. Darby was always there.

Darby was not just a good companion. He also brought me many smiles and special memories.

I was quite surprised to find him!

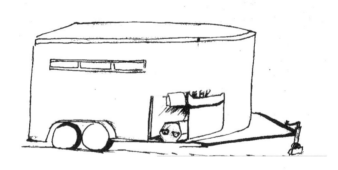

2

THE PURCHASE

Sometimes I went to horse sales. The horse sale in Great Falls, Montana was where I first met my wonderful horse Chick. I am glad I found her at that horse sale. Because of that I raised her wonderful children.

Horse sales are always exciting to attend. Sometimes I sold a horse at a sale. My brother was selling Blacky at the sale where I found Chick. Other times I bought horses at the sale. Sometimes I did both.

Often I went to horse sales in Missoula, Montana. One October sale was very eventful. Traveling through the Bitterroot Valley of Montana was spectacular. Trees were putting on their glorious Fall coats. The Bitterroot River was edged solid with colors of gold, orange, and yellow.

Excitement surrounded the sale area. The brisk air carried the smell of horses. I had to wear my coat and gloves to keep warm. The murmur of people floated over the horses' pens. People talked about each special horse. I loved them all!

Going into the sale ring, where horses are sold, I strolled by many horse trailers. Horse trailers are towed behind a vehicle, usually a pickup. Some are called gooseneck trailers. These have a big nose that hovers over the back of a truck. The trailer is hooked to the truck in the middle of the bed of the pickup. A bumper pull trailer tows behind the vehicle. It hooks onto the back bumper. A bumper pull could even be pulled by a car.

Nearing one trailer, I heard whining. I could not imagine what it was. The closer I got, the more I knew. There is a small enclosed area at the front of some trailers that holds saddles. This is called the tack compartment. Inside the cubby hole of this trailer were six little eyes staring at me. Three tiny puppies cried for attention. There was something strange about these eyes. While most dogs have black or brown eyes, these darling puppies had ice blue ones.

Not being able to resist, I had to go closer. They all wagged their fluffy short white tails. Yes, these puppies had very short tails. Their tails were short when the pups were born. All three of them wore long white coats. There were a few spots of blue and black on them. They were Blue-eyed White Australian Shepherds. This breed of dog is born to work sheep and cattle. They were born in Darby, Montana. Darby sits at the base of the Continental Divide. Lewis and Clark passed through this area on their trek.

One of the pups had very few blue spots. It was mostly white. This one was a little boy. When he wagged his furry tail, his whole body shook. He never took his eyes off me. I knew I could not leave without him. His owner wanted $50 for him. I went ahead and paid him.

Since the pups were born in Darby, that is what I named him. From then on, Darby never left my side. Wherever I went, he waddled along. When I got him home, he met up with a new friend he loved forever. Misty was my other dog. She was half golden retriever and half yellow lab. Darby adored her from the moment he met her. A few years later, Page was added to this circle of friends.

There was one time Darby followed I wished he had not. It almost cost him his life!

3

GETTING HURT

Darby went everyplace with me. He went even when he was tiny. He took a hundred baby steps to every one of mine.

One day Darby followed me down to the barn. It was a brisk morning. The mountains already wore their white top hats.

I was working with Onie. Onie was one of Chick's sons. His color was strawberry roan. This color of coat has red and white hairs mixed together. Onie was only a year old. He was rather cantankerous. I had him tied to the hitching post. This is a rail about four feet high. He did not like being tied up. He kept moving around. He pawed the ground with his front feet. "THUMP, THUMP, THUMP!" A deep hole formed in front of him. He was even mad at the air. He kicked at it with his hind feet. He also did not like me brushing him.

Darby played nearby while I worked with Onie. He whimpered, wanting to be next to me. I kept moving him back away from Onie.

I talked to Onie, trying to stroke his ears. Horses normally do not like their face and ears touched. Gently touching Onie's ears helped him. Then he would not be bothered by my putting his bridle on. I would do this when I was breaking him. To break a horse means train them to be ridden. While rubbing Onie's ears, I concentrated on his eyes. He watched me intently. He had not grown to trust me yet.

Inspecting Onie's eyes, I did not notice Darby's bad mistake. He walked right up to the back leg of Onie. You should never go behind any horse. Especially a young cantankerous one! Onie held his back leg up this whole time. This is a sure sign a horse will kick.

Before I got Darby out of the way, Onie's leg flew back. His hard hoof, or foot, hit Darby right in the head. Darby flew through the crisp air. 'PLUNK!!' His fur ball body landed on the frozen, hard ground. He did not move.

Sobbing, I ran to where he landed. He was hit hard in the head. I knew he was dead. As I reached down to him, he let out a soft whimper. He lifted his tiny head. His bright blue eyes carried a sad look for the first time.

Unbelievably, Darby did not get hurt. He was very scared, though. I carried him up the hill to the house. He wanted to stay in my arms. I hugged him for quite awhile. It was like hugging a soft pillow. I was so thankful he was alive.

With time, Darby got over his fright. He was more careful around the back feet of horses from that time on.

Darby's being kicked did not keep him from going on rides with me. It did not keep him from having fun, either!

4

SLEDDING

Darby loved to play. That never ended with him growing up. He played like a puppy even when he aged. He always looked like he had a smile on his face, too. I could not help but smile when he looked at me with his beautiful blue eyes. He never held back from wagging his tail when he looked at me. It happened spontaneously.

Darby loved the snow. The first time he saw it, he was just a few months old. He ran and fell on his belly with his legs stretched out. Off he slid on the icy bed. He was totally happy lying flat on the snow. Sometimes he rolled back and forth.

Darby liked playing in different ways. There was one thing he loved, though. That was sledding. He did not care if anyone else was on the sled. He loved jumping on and riding. If he could not get on the sled, he frolicked behind. Snow flew into his beaming face. He still bounded along.

Sometimes the hills we sledded on were very steep. Some had big mounds of sagebrush on them. Towering green fir trees lined others. We took a break from sledding, sometimes, to stand by the fire. Roasted hot dogs and marshmallows tasted best when the frozen snow surrounded us. Darby smelled like smoke from standing by the toasty fire. The glowing flames danced against the white snow. The heat from them comforted us.

There was a big steep hill near the house. We walked out to it. Our sleds skated behind. Hearing the scraping of them against the snow assured us they followed.

One of Darby's best friends was Snowball. He was a cat. His coat was short. He was mostly white. His head was cream colored. He had the same bright blue eyes as Darby.

Snowball always followed along. He liked to be with Darby. Even when we went riding horse, Snowball followed. In and out of the sagebrush he wove.

Once when we wanted to go sledding, there were bulls by the fence. This was the fence between our house and the hill. A bull is the father of a calf, a baby cow. I asked Darby to move the bulls away for us. Darby crouched down. He crept to the bulls. Right behind him was Snowball. Bounding up and down he went to assist Darby. The two of them accomplished the task. Misty watched with approval.

It was this same fence we counted 250 massive elk jumping over.

The elk is of the deer family. Once over, the elk proceeded to chase our horses. Needless to say, the horses were very frightened!

Nothing ever stopped Darby from sledding with us. Once he broke his front leg badly. He had to wear a small white cast. Even this did not stop him from sledding. He galloped behind the sled as fast as he could without the cast.

There was one thing Darby loved more than sledding!

5

RUNNING

Darby was born a cow dog. He loved to work cows. He got so excited when I saddled my horse. He knew he was going to get to work cows. If the trailer was hooked up to the pickup, Darby stood by it wagging his whole body.

Getting to ride in the back of the truck was almost as fun as working cows. Even though Misty was not a cow dog, she loved to tag along. The two of them stood on opposite sides of the bed of the truck. The wind made their ears fly back. Page was content sitting in the middle looking straight ahead. When the truck was parked, Page was usually found on top. She made sure everything was okay from her special throne!

Darby always stayed right beside my horse when I was riding. He only went to the cows when I told him to. He raced to the cattle when I said, "Ssst, get 'em up". Back and forth he ducked. Sometimes he even reached up and bit the cows' hind feet. The cows bellered and kicked at Darby. He was too fast for them, though. Darby nipped then scurried away.

If an ornery cow turned and snorted at Darby, he crouched down and stared the cow in the eye. There was no way that cow was going to intimidate Darby!

Darby rode miles and miles with my horses and me. He smiled and wagged his tail the whole way. It did not matter if we were in the mountains alongside the Continental Divide, riding to Bear Lakes out of Lemhi, Idaho, or riding across the sagebrush of Lemhi County. He was always beside me. I loved him being there. I did not appreciate, though, the time he put his front feet on Slick's shoulder causing him to buck with me!

Darby was happiest when there was a creek near us. He ran as fast as he could toward it. Then he sailed through the air. "SPLASH!" Into the middle of the creek he landed. Then he just lay there. Misty quite often was beside him when he did this. The icy mountain streams felt wonderful to him.

One time Darby and I were riding up Eight Mile Creek. This is on the Idaho side of the Divide. We had pushed cows to a different pasture. That way grass had a chance to grow where the cows had been eating. Once on top, we were in Montana. This day the cows and calves absolutely did not want to go. Gathering and moving them was a continual struggle. I could not have moved them without Darby. He ran and ran and ran around the cows. He kept them heading in the right direction.

Finally they were through the gate. We headed back to the truck. It was about a two-hour ride to it. We were in an open area on the top of the mountain. Blue, yellow, and pink wildflowers dotted the meadow. Darby was behind me just a little ways. He was quite worn out from all his hard work. When I looked back at him, he smiled and wagged at me as always. I noticed something lying beside him. I was amazed! There quietly rested a newborn baby elk.

The baby was invisible to Darby. When elk and deer are just born, they do not have a scent. That way predators like wolves cannot smell them.

Lying totally still is instinct, or the natural thing to do, for a baby elk. That way the predator will not see or hear it, either.

Taking my eye off the baby, I looked behind Darby. Charging after him was the baby's protective mother. I hollered at Darby to run faster. He stopped, sat down, and wagged his tail at me. The cow elk was just about ready to stomp on Darby when he got up and started running again. He did not even know she was behind him. He did

not hear very well. I hollered again, "Hurry up, Darby." "PLOP!!" He sat down. The elk was ready to stomp him again when he got up. The sitting down and getting up happened a few times. Then Darby saw her. He shot like a bullet. Right past me he zipped. I kicked my horse into a high lope. We finally got away from that loving mother. She was not very loving toward us!

This reminded me of the time when Darby chased the moose out of the cattails. My poor horse Barbie was scared to death! The timc Darby pushed a baby elk under my horse Junie was not nice either!

Although Darby caused me fright-ful moments, he had a scare no one should experience!

6

MISSING

Sometimes when we rode, Darby wandered a bit. This was especially so if Misty and Page were with us. They loved to dart through the brush and trees. If they were hot, they searched for a nippy creek to soak in.

Wandering got Darby into trouble sometimes. He could not see well because his eyes were so blue. Also, his not being able to hear well got him into trouble.

There were times Darby wandered too far away from us. When that happened, he could not find us. Then we went looking for him. We hollered and hollered. Finally he showed up. He wagged his tail and smiled the whole time. He did not know anything was wrong!

One of these times, though, we did not find Darby. We had ridden up Jake Canyon out of Leadore. The rocky canyon rose right behind our house. The canyon was narrow. The ride up it was rocky and steep. Our horses had to dig with their front feet to climb. Black Jack and Chick made this trek many times. They packed my sons, Cole and Gus, as little boys. A small stream fell down the mountain beside us.

Half of the way up a deep aqua pool sunk into the rocks.

Once we landed on top of the mountain, the view opened up. It was spectacular. We gazed through the fresh blue sky forever. The Lemhi Valley lay below us.

Near us rested a clear sparkling stream. Fish squiggled through the pristine water. Over and around the smooth rocks they swam.

There were no cows in this area so Darby played. He ran and ran. We kept riding. We enjoyed the beautiful surroundings. Once in awhile a deer or elk scurried behind thick pine trees in the distance.

The long ride wore us out. We did not notice Darby's absence. Misty wobbled in and out of the trees ahead of us.

Once we were home, we realized Darby was not with us. We called and called. He did not come. I knew he would show up anytime. I was wrong. Night fell upon us. Still no Darby. All the next day I watched for Darby. He did not show up. Another sad night came. I was very worried. I went looking for him the next day. Still I did not find him.

That night we were eating supper. It was hard to eat. I was so worried and sad. I looked out the window next to the dinner table. It seemed there was a little white dot far in the green field against the mountain. I figured I wanted Darby so badly I imagined it. I was relieved the little spot got bigger. It was Darby! He was sprinting off the mountain as fast as he could. His silky white coat flowed in the wind. His fluff ball tail never stopped wagging.

When Darby got to the house, I asked, "What have you been doing the last two days?" He did not answer. He probably did not even realize he was lost!

We were glad to get Darby back. One time we almost didn't!

7

TAKEN

Darby's disappearing scared me. I worried he would not show up. I could not imagine not seeing Darby again.

One day we rode to Mill Lake. I was riding Leroy. Darby and Misty sprinted happily along. Page was still a baby. She rode on the horses with us. It was a fall day. Mill Creek was not roaring as in the spring. The mountain top had already sent its white cap down with the warm summer air. Warm spring weather melts mountain snow causing streams to fill to their fullest. The hot summer air melts caps of snow on the very tops of the giants.

Just past the start of the trail, we passed some hunters. We even stopped and visited for awhile. I noticed one hunter's pickup was just like mine, only white. It had a Utah license plate on it.

After visiting, we continued our journey. We were warmed by the sun. The day was perfect. The placid mountain lake was beautiful. Rocky walls rose out of the edge of it. The lake held their reflection. The weather was nice. The companionship was great!

The day after we rode, I went to check on Chick, Barbie, Goldie, and Tawny. They were in the 'Rock Pile' pasture. Hundreds of quaking aspen trees provided shelter for the mares (female horses). The quakies waved their little golden hands in the breeze.

The Rock Pile was near where we rode to Mill Lake. I drove the pickup to get there. The mares were close and I drove slowly. Darby and Misty ran behind. Page slept in the truck. Tall, glistening quaking aspen lined the dirt road. Darby and Misty were careful to stay out of the dust from the rolling tires.

After I got home, I only saw Misty and Page. Sometimes Darby found a dark place to curl up and sleep. I wondered if he was taking a nap. Quite often he howled in his sleep. I did not hear him doing this.

Time passed and I realized Darby was again missing. We went looking for him. We did not find him. We searched and searched. Still, we did not find him.

Many of the neighbors knew Darby. He was always with me. I asked them if they had seen him. No one had. I was getting more and more scared.

I had one neighbor to ask yet. He said a hunter from Utah had stopped. The neighbor noticed a dog that looked like Darby in the back of the hunter's truck. I about dropped to my knees. Could Darby have been kidnapped? Maybe he thought the hunter's truck was ours.

One of the local ranchers knew the hunter's name. After over a month of investigating, I finally found

Darby. Darby was 700 miles away in Southern Utah with the hunter. He had been kidnapped.

I fought and fought to get Darby back. The hunter did not want to give him back to me. He had grown to love him. Who wouldn't! Finally, the hunter delivered Darby to Idaho Falls, Idaho. This was still 160 miles away.

I was relieved Darby was finally safe. This thought came too soon. By the time we got to Idaho Falls to pick up Darby, Cole, Gus, and I were ecstatic. The long trip seemed to take forever. It had been months since we had seen our beloved friend. We missed him so much. We cried often. We thought we would never see him again.

Rushing to see Darby, we felt the greatest letdown of our lives. Darby had run away. He must have been confused being in a new place. The situation probably frightened him. We searched and searched, once again, for him. The city of Idaho Falls would not let him go. Sadly, we went home without Darby.

A friend worked at the animal shelter in Idaho Falls. Ken promised he would keep an eye out for Darby. All we could do was hope.

One wonderful morning I received a phone call. Darby had been found. Problems continued after the phone call. I still had to fight to get Darby back.

After three months of our hearts not being complete, Darby was with us. Darby, Cole, Gus, Misty, Page, Snowball, and I were all happy again.

We kept a close eye on Darby after he was kidnapped. There was something, though, that made it tough for us!

8

AFRAID

Guarding Darby was very hard during one time of the year. He was scared to death of fireworks. There could never be anything that frightened him more. A mad cow elk did not bother him as much as fireworks.

I protected Darby when fireworks were used. I felt so sorry for him. There was no comfort I could give him. He whined and shook when lights screeched through the air. I was thankful his hearing was not the best. The loud whistle and scream would have been worse for him had he been able to hear well.

When Darby disappeared during the uproar, I usually knew where to find him. One time, though, was different.

Darby had disappeared once again. The "POP, POP, POP!!" had been extreme earlier. I looked and looked for Darby. He was nowhere. I asked many of the neighbors. They had not seen him either.

I drove past one neighbor's house. The neighbor's pickup was parked outside. His pickup was just like mine. I glanced at the back of the truck. Barely visible was a hairy head. It was Darby.

A place Darby always felt safe was in the back of my truck. His fear of the fireworks caused him to run off. When he saw this pickup, he thought it was mine. In he jumped and hid.

When I called to Darby, he sat up

straighter. Looking over the bed of the truck, his whole body started wagging. His smiling blue eyes threw a loving glance my way. He was filled with joy. One thing Darby could do was hug. He gave me the biggest hug ever.

Although he was satisfied being in the wrong truck, he was much more relieved to be in mine. I was too!

I took Darby home. I tried to help him get through the fireworks season. It was a relief for both of us when the clamor was over for the year. I knew Darby would not be so terrified for another twelve months!

Even though Darby had some trying and scary times, there was something in his life that gave him much happiness!

9

A DAD

Darby loved playing, running, working cows, visiting people, and spending time with his friends. One thing that Darby really loved, though, was seeing his own children.

Darby was a father to many babies. He and Page were the parents of these special children. The babies were all so different.

Darby had what is called a naturally docked tail. This means his tail was short. Most of his children's tails were short like his. Many of the babies had long hair like their father's. Some of the children wore Page's short-haired coat.

Quite a few of the puppies inherited Darby's striking blue eyes. Only one of them was mostly white like Darby. That was Ruby.

Darby's babies were all different colors, too. Some were blue with black spots. Others were red with white around their necks. A couple of them looked like little rotweiller dogs. They must have gotten this look from Page. They were all roly-poly babies!

As soon as the babies were born, Darby took an interest in them. He did not want to bother Page. He admired the babies from a distance. I think he learned his lesson about an angry mother from the elk.

The puppies' eyes opened about two weeks after they were born. Darby then got a little closer to them. By the time the puppies were a month old, they were ready to play. Darby never acted like a father to them. He acted liked a playful friend. They knew he was their father, though. They liked to follow him around as soon as they could.

When Darby sat down, all the babies surrounded him. They frolicked, played, and tumbled over each other around him. The puppies even crawled on top of him. He loved the attention.

It was fun listening to the babies yipping. Sometimes they even barked and growled. Other times they whined, telling their mom they needed her. When little Brutus first felt cold snow on his soft pink paws he sat down. With his nose straight in the air, he howled like his dad. Brutus' long coat was grey and black.

Darby did what a father should do. He was always there for his children. He protected them.

The love Darby showed his children was the same love he showed everyone else. This was the strongest love anyone could have known!

10

A FRIEND

It was dangerous for a person to get his or her face close to Darby's. Darby, with his scratchy tongue, immediately gave a kiss. He never gave a little kiss. It was always a humongous one. Even to a stranger. He loved everyone.

Darby never left my side. He stayed by the door until I told him it was time to go to bed. He slept under my bedroom window.

When he howled in his sleep, I gently called his name. A loving glance slipped from his sleepy eyes.

If Darby could not be by me, he was by my horse. If my horse was not around, he stayed in the truck. He was never far from what he thought was mine.

Darby only cost me $50. He was worth a million dollars. He was the best companion I could ever have.

I wish everyone could experience just once a loving fun friendship like I had with Darby. Then you could feel beautiful blue eyes saying, "I Love You!"

^ZC HORSES SERIES

You have finally gotten to meet Chick and her children's faithful companion, Darby. Next you will meet Chick's beautiful daughter, Sonny! Learn how striking in appearance she was! Find out what terrible thing happened when she was first ridden! See what kind of personality she had! You will love her after you read the tenth book in the **'ZC HORSES'** series, *"Sonny-The Spectacular"*. Be sure to be there to greet her!!

^ZC HORSES SERIES #10
Sonny-The Spectacular
by Diane W. Keaster

Coming Spring 2006

To My Reader:

I was born and raised on a ranch near a little town called Belt, Montana. After receiving my B.S. in Business Education from Montana State University, I taught high school business. I then moved on to other facets of employment.

The whole time, I was team roping and raising, breaking, and training horses. The profession I fell into by mistake was trading horses. Throughout my life I have handled hundreds of horses, all which have a story of their own.

My sons, Cole and Augustus, loved reading stories about horses when they were small and I loved reading the stories to them. That is why I am writing these books. I want to tell the stories of the creatures I love to the children I love.

I thank Jehovah our Creator for giving us such a wonderful, beautiful animal!

Enjoy the stories!

Order Form
ZC HORSES SERIES

Don't miss out on any part of the lives of Chick and her many babies and friends! Experience all of the rides, joys and sorrows. Don't be left out!

___ Chick-The Beginning! (Spring 2001)	$6.95
___ Chick-The Saddle Horse! (Summer 2001)	$6.95
___ Chick-The Mom! (March 2002)	$6.95
___ Luke-The First! (July 2002)	$6.95
___ Barbie-The Best! (Oct. 2002)	$6.95
___ Leroy-The Prize (Summer 2003)	$6.95
___ Goldie-The Wise (February 2004)	$6.95
___ Chickadee-The Traveler (September 2004)	$6.95
___ Darby-The Cow Dog (October 2005)	$6.95
___ Sonny-The Spectacular (Spring 2006)	$6.95
___ Appaloosa-The State Horse (Summer 2006)	$6.95

UPCOMING TITLES

Tawny-The Beauty!	Black Jack-The Great!
Onie-The Roanie!	Belle-The Sweetie!
Classy-The Special!	Lily-The Pretty Paint!
Slick-The Friend!	Apple-The Joy!

Also read about Cider, Buck, Nellie, Junie, Eagle, Smokey, Sarge, Tex, Radar and many more!

ZC HORSES SERIES, 8 Hokanson Ln, Salmon, ID 83467
(208) 756-3757
www.zc-horses.com Email: zchorses@hotmail.com
Please send me the books I have checked above. I am enclosing US $____(please add $2/bk or $4/order, whichever is less, to cover shipping and handling).

NAME_____

ADDRESS_____

CITY/STATE/ZIP_____
PHONE_____
E-MAIL_____

Please allow four to six weeks for delivery. Shipping prices good in U.S. only. Prices subject to change.